Italian Sabre Martial Art

The Tradition and the Tecnique

Published by Giovanni Ricco

~~~~

Rev 1.1
~~~~

Content

Introduction

In the annals of martial arts, the 19th-century sabre occupies a unique place, especially within the Italian context. During this era, the sabre was not just a weapon; it was an emblem of martial prowess, used extensively in military engagements and duels. As the century progressed, the martial art of sabre fencing began its metamorphosis into a sport, marking a period when techniques and tactics reached unparalleled sophistication.

This book is designed as a bridge, connecting the intricate, revered manuals of yesteryears with the needs and aspirations of today's students. While the original manuals, penned by esteemed fencing masters, were primarily crafted for instructors, this guide endeavors to simplify and distill their essence. By highlighting core techniques and presenting them through annotated photo sequences, we aim to make these methods more digestible and accessible for the modern learner.

Our focus isn't merely on technique. A substantial portion of this book delves into the rich historical and cultural tapestry that underpins this martial art. Through this, readers gain not just technical proficiency but a holistic understanding of the art's context and evolution.

The objective is not to replace the original works but to complement them. By offering an integrated approach to the two predominant fencing methods of the 19th century, this book stands as a testament to the masters' legacy, making their wisdom more accessible and relevant for contemporary enthusiasts.

In essence, this guide is more than a technical manual; it's an invitation to journey through time, to understand the nuances, strategies, and philosophies that defined an era of fencing. As you delve deeper, you'll not only learn the techniques but also appreciate the contrasts and commonalities between the distinct combat styles of the 19th century.

Historical Significance of the Italian Duelling Sabre

The Italian Duelling Sabre, also known as the Sciabola de Duello or Sciabola di Terreno, played a crucial role in the history of civilian duelling from the mid-19th to the 20th century. The development of this weapon in Italy during the second half of the 19th century marked a significant shift in the culture of duelling, as it was crafted specifically for the purpose of civilian duelling rather than for military use (Parise, 1884), (Radaelli, 1885).

Unlike the military sabre, the Italian Duelling Sabre was a cutting and thrusting weapon specifically intended for duelling. It shared construction elements and a general shape with other sabres, but its theory and purpose were distinct. Its slightly curved blade was wider at the end near the guard and gradually tapered toward the point. The blade also had fullers (grooves) along the sides, which extended from the end of the blade forward to approximately one third from the point. The last section of the blade became flat. Both the true edge and the back edge were sharpened and ran back one-third from the point along the spine. The point could be sharpened or rounded.

The Italian Duelling Sabre was also built with a guard made with a knuckle bow of a variety of shapes designed to cover and protect the hand from both cuts and thrusts. The grips were often wrapped with sharkskin and wire, and a back strap made of steel that was checkered ran along the top of the grip. The training sabre was a blunted version of the duelling weapon and had a slender grip made of wood that could be carved, checkered, or wound with cord, leather, and wire.

A hallmark of the Italian styles of fencing, including the use of the duelling sabre, is the emphasis on the point over cutting. This approach has been stressed since the time of the Roman legions and reflects the principles of fencing that underpin many methods of Italian stick fighting. However, despite the dual capability of the Italian Duelling Sabre for both cutting and thrusting, thrusts were often prohibited in duels.

The Italian Duelling Sabre is considered to be mostly straight or with minimal curvature, differing from the more curved sabres typically associated with cavalry use. While it shares a similar "genome" with the modern sabre, there are notable differences in its design and use.

In conclusion, the Italian Duelling Sabre was an emblem of the culture of duelling during the second half of the 19th century and into the 20th century. It represented a unique fusion of form, function, and tradition, reflecting the historical significance of fencing in Italy and the evolution of the art of duelling.

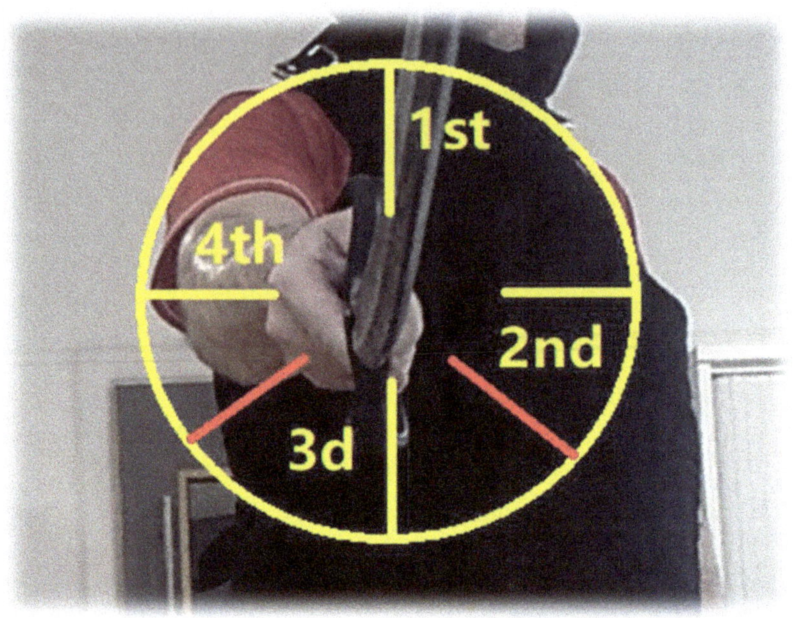

1st
2nd
3d
4th

Comparative analysis: Sword vs. Sabre Fencing

The world of fencing is a rich tapestry of techniques, styles, and weapons. Among the most iconic and storied of these weapons are the sword and the sabre. While both are bladed instruments designed for combat, their use, history, and techniques differ in several key ways. This chapter delves into the nuances that distinguish sword fencing from sabre fencing, shedding light on the unique dance of each weapon.

Sword (Rapier):

The rapier, with its slender and pointed blade, is a weapon that epitomizes the art of finesse in fencing. Its design emphasizes thrusting, and its techniques are built around precision, agility, and control. Here's a deeper dive into the stance and techniques associated with rapier fencing:

Stance: The stance for rapier fencing is upright and poised. The front foot points directly at the opponent, while the back foot is positioned at a right angle. This stance provides a stable base, essential for the rapid lunges and retreats characteristic of rapier play. The weapon arm is extended straight from the shoulder, with the tip of the rapier aimed at the opponent, ready to exploit any openings.

Thrusts: The primary mode of attack with the rapier is the thrust. Given the weapon's slender design, thrusts are quick and can be directed at various targets, from the opponent's torso to their extremities. The goal is to strike with accuracy, exploiting gaps in the opponent's defence.

Parries: Defence with the rapier is often minimalistic yet effective. Parries are designed to redirect the opponent's blade just enough to allow for a counterthrust. Given the rapier's length and flexibility, parries can be executed with a small movement, allowing for quick transitions between defence and offense.

Footwork: Mobility is key in rapier fencing. Quick advances, measured retreats, and sudden lunges are all integral to the style. The footwork is precise, ensuring that the fencer remains balanced, whether they're on the offensive or evading an opponent's attack.

Feints and Deception: Given the rapier's focus on precision, feints—deceptive movements designed to elicit a response from the opponent—are a crucial part of its techniques. A well-executed feint can draw out a parry from the opponent, creating an opening for a genuine attack.

The rapier, with its emphasis on precision and control, offers a unique fencing experience. Every movement, from the positioning of the feet to the extension of the arm, is calculated. It's a dance of strategy and skill, where understanding distance, timing, and the opponent's intentions can mean the difference between landing a hit or being struck.

Sabre:

Sabre fencing is characterized by its fluidity and rhythm. The curved blade of the sabre lends itself to sweeping, slashing attacks, and the techniques reflect this.

Stance: The typical sabre stance is side-on, with the front foot pointing at the opponent and the back foot perpendicular. This stance allows for rapid advances and retreats, essential for the cut-and-thrust nature of sabre fencing.

Cuts: Sabre cuts come from various angles — overhead (head cuts), from the side (slashing cuts to the flank or arm), and even from below (rising cuts). The curved blade allows for a natural slicing motion, making these cuts particularly effective.

Thrusts: While the sabre is primarily a cutting weapon, it's still capable of delivering effective thrusts. These are often used as surprise attacks, exploiting openings left by an opponent's failed cut or parry.

Parries: In sabre fencing, parries are active and dynamic. Instead of just blocking an opponent's blade, the goal is to redirect it, creating an opening for a riposte. Given the sabre's cutting nature, parries must be precise to prevent the blade from simply sliding off and completing its cut.

Footwork: Given the aggressive nature of sabre fencing, footwork is crucial. Quick advances, rapid retreats, and sudden lunges are all part of a sabreur's toolkit. The ability to change direction swiftly, combined with the dynamic nature of the weapon, makes sabre fencing a fast-paced and thrilling discipline.

In both sword and sabre fencing, understanding distance and timing is crucial. The techniques, while different in execution, all aim to exploit openings while minimizing exposure to counterattacks. The dance of these weapons is a blend of strategy, skill, and athleticism.

Comparative Analysis of Duelling Sabre Styles - Italian versus Polish, British, German, and French Styles

Italian Style:

The Italian duelling sabre style, also known as the Radaellian style, focuses on linear and direct movements. The Italian style emphasizes precision, speed, and timing, with a strong emphasis on the thrust. The weapon is held in a high guard, often with the hand at or above shoulder height, and attacks are typically delivered from this high guard position. The Italian style also encourages fluid movement, with the fencer stepping forward to attack and backward to defend, maintaining a safe distance from the opponent at all times.

Polish Style:

Polish sabre fencing, also known as "szabla", is a more circular and fluid style compared to the Italian style. The emphasis is on cutting rather than thrusting, and the style includes a lot of circular parries and sweeping cuts. The guard position in the Polish style is often lower than in the Italian style, with the hand held at waist height. This style is highly dynamic and incorporates a lot of movement, including jumps and spins.

British Style:

The British style, often associated with the military sabre, is a balanced blend of cut and thrust techniques. The guard position is typically at chest height, and the style emphasizes control, timing, and distance. The British style also includes a variety of guard positions and encourages the fencer to change guards in response to the opponent's actions.

German Style:

The German style, known as "Mensur", uses a unique type of sabre called a "schlager". This style is a blend of cut and thrust techniques, with a particular emphasis on thrusting. The guard position is typically at chest height, similar to the British style. The German style is known for its precision and discipline, with fencers often remaining stationary and focusing on accuracy and timing rather than movement.

French Style:

The French style of sabre fencing is characterized by its elegance and fluidity. This style emphasizes agility and speed, with a focus on swift, direct attacks and quick parries. The French style encourages a lot of movement, with the fencer often advancing and retreating quickly to control the distance with the opponent. The guard position is typically at shoulder height, and the style includes a variety of complex guard positions and techniques.

The Evolution of Italian Sabre Fencing in the XIX Century

The art of Italian sabre fencing in the 19th century was a dynamic and evolving discipline, marked by the emergence of distinct schools of thought and influential figures. Two of the most prominent masters of this era were Giuseppe Radaelli and Masaniello Parise, whose contrasting philosophies and techniques shaped the landscape of Italian fencing.

Giuseppe Radaelli, hailing from Milan, revolutionized the traditional fencing approach with his advocacy for a lighter, more agile sabre. His style emphasized speed, agility, and wide sweeping cuts, deviating from the thrust-centric techniques that had dominated Italian fencing. His methods, developed in the mid to late 19th century, were not only adopted by the Italian military in the 1860s but also found relevance in duelling contexts, where honour was often at stake.

On the other hand, Masaniello Parise, a Neapolitan master and director of the prestigious "Scuola Magistrale Militare" di Scherma in Rome, championed the classical Italian fencing approach. His teachings emphasized precision, control, and the primacy of thrusts over cuts. The depth and strategy inherent in Parise's method eventually led to its adoption as the official manual for the Royal Italian Army, marking a significant victory for the traditional Italian school of fencing.

However, the story doesn't end with the rivalry between Radaelli and Parise. One of Radaelli's most distinguished students, Luigi Barbasetti, carried the torch of his master's teachings beyond Italy's borders. Settling in Hungary, Barbasetti introduced Radaelli's techniques, which were warmly embraced and melded with local strategies. This amalgamation laid the foundation for the Eastern European fencing style, a unique blend that would come to dominate the region's fencing scene.

Both the Radaelli and Parise manuals, while rooted in their distinct philosophies, offer a comprehensive understanding of Italian sabre fencing's multifaceted nature. They serve as invaluable resources for anyone delving into historical fencing, encapsulating a rich tapestry of techniques, tactics, and principles that remain pertinent even today.

In essence, the evolution of the Italian duelling sabre in the 19th century is a testament to the fluidity and dynamism of martial arts. It's a narrative of innovation, rivalry, and the dissemination of ideas across borders. The enduring legacies of Radaelli, Parise, and Barbasetti continue to resonate in modern fencing, underscoring their indelible impact on the discipline.

Styles Competition

The competition between Radaelli and Parise was a spectacle that drew the attention of the entire Italian fencing community. It was not merely a contest of skill but a clash of philosophies, a battle between the old and the new, the traditional and the innovative.

Radaelli, with his dynamic, cut-centric style, was the first to present. His sabre, lighter and nimbler than the traditional weapons, moved like an extension of his body. He demonstrated a series of wide, sweeping cuts, each one executed with a speed and fluidity that left the audience in awe. His footwork was agile, his movements unpredictable, embodying the essence of his philosophy - fencing as an art of motion and unpredictability.

His style was a stark contrast to the traditional methods, emphasizing the cut over the thrust, the dynamic over the static. It was a daring departure from the norm, a bold statement that challenged the very foundations of Italian fencing.

Next was Parise, a stalwart of the traditional Italian school of fencing. His style was measured, precise, a study in control and strategy. He demonstrated a series of thrusts, each one executed with pinpoint accuracy. His footwork was deliberate, his movements calculated, embodying the essence of his philosophy - fencing as a game of strategy and control.

Parise's style was a testament to the traditions of Italian fencing. It emphasized the thrust over the cut, the strategic over the dynamic. It was a reaffirmation of the established norms, a powerful statement that upheld the very foundations of Italian fencing.

The panel, composed of military officials and fencing masters, deliberated long and hard. They considered the merits of both styles, the innovation of Radaelli's approach against the tradition of Parise's. In the end, they decided in favour of Parise's method.

The panel cited the strategic depth and control of Parise's style as key factors in their decision. They believed that his approach, with its emphasis on precision and strategy, was better suited to the needs of the Royal Italian Army. This decision marked a significant victory for the traditional Italian school of fencing and solidified Parise's influence on the future of Italian fencing.

However, the competition was more than just a contest between two masters. It was a defining moment in the history of Italian fencing, a moment that highlighted the tension between tradition and innovation, the old and the new. It was a moment that would shape the future of Italian fencing for generations to come.

Type of Duels

Duelling in Italy during the late 19th century was influenced by a variety of social, cultural, and political factors. While duelling had been a part of European culture for centuries, the practice underwent significant changes during the 19th century. Here are some key features of Italian duels during this period:

1. Formal Duelling Code: By the late 19th century, duelling in Italy was regulated by a formal code, the Italian Code Duello, which dictated the rules and procedures of the duel. This code set out the acceptable reasons for a duel, how a challenge should be issued, the role of seconds, and how the duel itself should be conducted.

2. Reasons for Duelling: Duels were often fought over matters of honour. Insults, accusations of cheating, and personal slights could all lead to a challenge. It was also common for duels to occur due to romantic disputes or professional rivalries.

3. Weapons Used: The Italian duelling sabre was the most commonly used weapon in duels during this period. It was a lightweight, single-edged weapon designed for thrusting and cutting. Other weapons, such as pistols, could also be used, but the sabre was the preferred weapon of choice.

4. Participants: Participants in a duel were typically members of the upper classes, including nobles, military officers, and wealthy merchants. Duelling was seen as a gentleman's activity, and participating in a duel could enhance

one's social status. However, duels could also involve individuals from different social classes.

5. Outcome of Duels: The aim of a duel was not necessarily to kill the opponent, but rather to restore one's honour by demonstrating courage and skill. Many duels ended after first blood was drawn or a clear hit was landed. However, fatalities did occur in some cases.

6. Location of Duels: Duels were often held at dawn in secluded locations to avoid interruption and potential legal repercussions. Common locations included gardens, parks, and on occasion, indoors in private estates.

7. Legal Status: Duelling was officially illegal in many parts of Italy during this period, and participants could face legal penalties. However, laws against duelling were often not strictly enforced, particularly when the duellists were members of the upper classes.

8. Cultural Significance: Despite its illegality, duelling was deeply ingrained in Italian culture during the 19th century. It was seen as a test of courage, skill, and honour, and was often romanticized in literature and the popular imagination.

The Sabre in Battle: A Dominant Weapon of the Mid-19th Century

The 19th century was a period of significant military evolution, with tactics, strategies, and weaponry undergoing substantial changes. Among the weapons of this era, the sabre stood out, especially in the first half of the century, as a preferred choice for both infantry and cavalry units. Its design and intended use were distinct from other bladed weapons, making it particularly suited for the chaotic environment of the battlefield.

Design and Intended Use

The sabre's design was a testament to its utility in battle. Unlike rapiers and traditional straight swords, which were primarily thrusting weapons, the sabre was designed for slashing. Its curved blade allowed for powerful, sweeping cuts, capable of delivering debilitating or fatal wounds. This slashing capability was especially crucial in the heat of battle, where the objective was not just to wound, but to halt an advancing enemy. While a rapier's thrust could be lethal, it lacked the immediate stopping power of a heavy sabre cut, which could incapacitate an opponent instantly.

Sabre vs. Rapier and Sword in Battle

In the crowded and tumultuous environment of 19th-century warfare, soldiers often faced multiple adversaries simultaneously. In such scenarios, the ability to swing a weapon in wide arcs, potentially striking multiple opponents, was invaluable. A thrusting weapon like the rapier, while deadly in one-on-one duels, lacked the same efficacy in the chaos of a battlefield.

The sabre's design allowed soldiers to engage multiple foes, making it a more versatile weapon in large-scale conflicts.

Infantry vs. Cavalry Sabres

While the sabre was a staple for both infantry and cavalry, there were notable differences in design between the two. The cavalry sabre was more curved, optimized for slashing from horseback. The momentum of a mounted soldier, combined with the curve of the blade, could deliver devastating cuts.

On the other hand, the infantry sabre was less curved, reflecting its dual role in both slashing and thrusting. For foot soldiers, the ability to thrust was still crucial, especially in close combat scenarios where there might be less room to swing the weapon. Additionally, the infantry sabre came into play when primary weapons, like rifles, were rendered unusable, either due to malfunction, breakage, or when ammunition was exhausted.

Martial Arts and the Sabre

Beyond its primary use as a weapon, the sabre also found its place in martial arts. In close combat, soldiers trained in martial techniques could use their unarmed hand to grab opponents, either seizing their limbs or even their weapons. This tactic was combined with wrestling moves to disarm, incapacitate, or gain a positional advantage over the enemy. However, it's worth noting that many of these techniques, while practiced, were not extensively detailed in the primary Italian manuals referenced for this book. As a result, they aren't discussed in-depth or illustrated within its pages.

In conclusion the sabre's prominence in the 19th-century battlefield was no accident. Its design, tailored for the realities of war, made it a weapon of choice for soldiers across different military roles. Its legacy, both as a tool of war and a martial arts weapon, underscores its versatility and effectiveness in an era of rapid military evolution.

The Weapon

The hardware features of the Italian duelling sabre from the 19th century:

The duelling sabre was a cutting and thrusting weapon specifically intended for civilian duelling. Its theory and purpose were developed in Italy during the second half of the 19th century. The slightly curved blade is wider at the end near the guard and gradually tapers toward the point. The blade also has a true edge and a back edge that runs back one-third from the point along the spine and both are sharpened. The point could be sharpened or rounded.

Along the sides of the blade are fullers (grooves), which extend from the end of the blade forward to approximately one third from the point. This last section of the blade becomes flat.

The sabre is constructed with a guard made with a knuckle bow that can be of a variety of shapes designed to cover and protect the hand from both cuts and thrusts.

These sabres often had grips that were wrapped with sharkskin and wire and a back strap made of steel that was checkered which ran along the top of the grip.

The training sabre was a blunted version of the duelling weapon. It consisted of a blade that during its forging was often times folded over into a blunt point which was nearly square in shape. It had a slender grip made of wood that could be carved, checkered, wound with cord, leather and wire or cord, leather and wire as well as the sharkskin version previously mentioned.

The Italian duelling sabre is mostly straight or with a minimal curvature, while the more curved sabres indicated more a use for chivalry.

Type of Sabre for training

Training Sabres: A Comparative Analysis

Sabre training in Historical European Martial Arts (HEMA) involves the use of different types of training sabres, each with its unique advantages and limitations. It is essential to understand the characteristics of these training tools and the safety measures necessary when using them.

1. Metal Sabres

Metal sabres closely replicate the weight and size of real weapons used in duels, making them the most authentic training tools. Their bladeless design and rounded or blunted tips offer a certain degree of safety while still providing a realistic fencing experience. However, using a metal sabre requires rigorous safety precautions, including protective gear like fencing masks, jackets, and gloves.

Pros:

- Provides the most authentic training experience due to its weight and size similarity to real weapons.

- Rounded or blunted tips ensure safety during sparring sessions.

Cons:

- Might not be suitable for beginners due to its weight. Beginners need time to develop appropriate muscle strength to handle these sabres effectively.

- Requires comprehensive safety gear to avoid injuries.

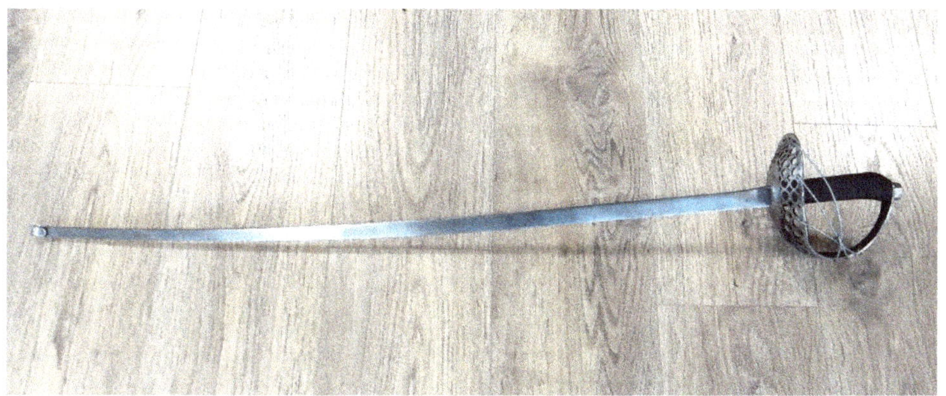

2. **Sabre Replicas**

Sabre replicas come with sharp blades and tips, closely resembling the real weapons used in duels. These sabres can provide a realistic feel during standalone training sessions. However, due to their sharpness, they are not recommended for sparring or training with partners.

Pros:

- Offers a highly realistic feel due to the sharp blades and tips.

- Suitable for standalone training to understand the weapon's handling.

Cons:

- Not recommended for partner training due to the potential risk of injury.

- Use might be restricted or illegal in some regions due to their sharpness.

3. **Synthetic Sabres**

Synthetic sabres offer a balanced compromise between authenticity and safety. Their weight is similar to real weapons, and they are sufficiently rigid with the correct length. Synthetic sabres are suitable for both individual and partner training sessions.

Pros:

- Good balance between the realistic feel and safety considerations.

- Suitable for both individual and partner training.

- Requires less extensive safety gear compared to metal sabres.

Cons:

- Despite being safer than metal sabres, they still require protective gear such as fencing masks, jackets, and gloves.

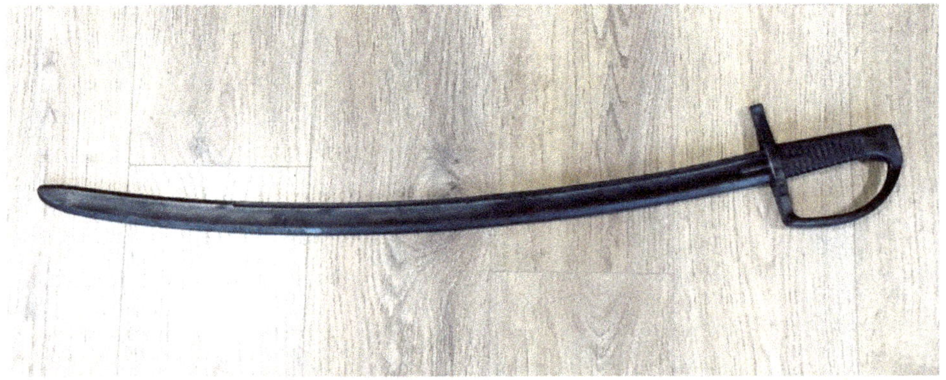

4. **Padded Sabres**

Padded sabres are the safest training tools, making them ideal for beginners or low-intensity training sessions. However, their design does not replicate the sliding feature of curved weapons, and they lack the weight of real sabres, limiting their effectiveness for advanced training.

Pros:

- The safest option for sabre training, suitable for beginners.

- Requires minimal protective gear.

Cons:

- Lacks the sliding feature of curved weapons, limiting their effectiveness in training.

- Does not provide the realistic weight feel of a real sabre.

In conclusion, the choice of training sabre should be based on the fencer's skill level, training intensity, and the safety measures available. Beginners might find synthetic or padded sabres more suitable, while advanced fencers could benefit from the realistic feel of metal sabres or sabre replicas for standalone training. Regardless of the tool, safety should always be the priority, and the use of appropriate protective gear is crucial.

Personalizing your Sabre

The primary thing to remember is that not all sabres are created equal.
Often, practitioners find themselves using a sabre not precisely designed for
the style they intend to employ.

From the manuals, we gather insights on how sabres should be constructed
to be effective both for duels and battlefield combat. It's crucial to remember
that these manuals were primarily conceived for battlefield combat. Yet, they
are so meticulously crafted that the techniques described were also
employed in the duels of the time, which reached their pinnacle in Italy
around the turn of the 20th century.

A sabre should be balanced four fingers away from the guard. In other words,
when holding the weapon with the palm of the hand and the little finger
touching the guard, it should balance on the index finger. Few metal sabres
achieve this balance; most are balanced six fingers away. This means the
sabre will be slower in thrusts, parries, and other actions but will have a more
substantial impact when used forcefully to attack the opponent's weapon or
to deliver a cutting blow.

To counteract this imbalance, one can add weight using wire or small metal
blocks to the rear part of the weapon, shifting the centre of gravity backward.
It's worth noting that while adding mass improves the weapon's balance, it
also increases its weight, which can tire the fencer when in a resting position.

The best approach is to add weight to balance the weapon as required, test it in sparring, and then gradually remove some weight to find the right balance between weight and balance that satisfies the fencer. The two parameters to consider are the four-finger balance and a weight as close to 800 grams as possible. Ideally, one should approach both these parameters without compromising one for the other. Any added weight should not in any way hinder hand and wrist movement, especially during thrusts. In such cases, the forearm and wrist align with the weapon's handle and can interfere with the added mass, limiting hand movement and reducing the effectiveness of the thrust. The additional weight should be positioned low enough below the guard's nut to avoid this interference.

It's also essential to note that many HEMA competitions do not allow this modification. So, be prepared to forgo this added weight if you decide to use the weapon in tournaments. The weight addition should be modular, easy to adjust, and stable enough to prevent loosening during training. While it shouldn't pose a safety concern, it's certainly not ideal for a weapon to shed parts, even if they're located behind the palm.

Another crucial aspect of the sabre is the rigid guard protection. Exposing the hand, especially the inner part, to blows can be hazardous. Current fencing gloves offer decent protection mainly on the hand's outer part. It's not uncommon to be struck on a less protected part, like the palm. To enhance this protection, one can add wire connecting the upper and lower parts of the guard. It's worth noting that the manuals anticipate this and include additional side protections for the hand. Importantly, the side protection should not restrict the hand's rotational movement in any way. Remember, wrist movement, especially in duelling sabres, is vital.

Protections for Sabre Training

Safety Protections for Free Sparring with Metal Sabre.

It's remarkable that the use of protective gear during training was already considered in the late 19th century. Typically, fencers wore fencing masks, gloves made from thick shoe leather, and jackets. It was also common to use bladeless and blunted sabres.

Head

The head is one of the most critical areas to protect in sabre fencing. A fencing mask is a must-have item. It should cover the entire head, face, and neck, and it must meet the safety standards. The mask should have a bib that protects the neck and is made of puncture-resistant fabric. Some fencers also choose to use a mask overlay or additional padding for extra protection against high-impact strikes.

Torso

To protect the torso, a fencing jacket is necessary. The jacket should be puncture-resistant and cover the torso and arms completely. Underneath the jacket, a protective plastron (or underarm protector) is worn on the weapon arm side to provide an additional layer of protection. For male fencers, a protective cup is also strongly recommended. Some fencers choose to wear a chest protector, particularly in women's fencing.

Arms

The arms, like the torso, are covered by the fencing jacket, providing puncture resistance. For additional protection, especially during free sparring with a metal sabre, it's advisable to consider using elbow protectors. These are rigid protective guards designed to safeguard the elbow joint from direct strikes, and they are often made from materials like hard plastic or foam. They should fit securely without restricting movement, and they are typically secured with adjustable straps for a snug fit.

In addition to the elbow protectors, fencers should wear a glove on the weapon hand that extends halfway up the forearm to protect the hand and lower arm. Some fencing gloves are specially designed to offer additional padding and protection against hits. The non-weapon arm does not require a glove but is still covered by the jacket.

Hands

The hands are particularly vulnerable in fencing and require special protection. A sturdy glove is worn on the weapon hand, offering protection against hits and blisters. The glove should be made of tough, durable material and should fit well, allowing for full movement of the hand and fingers. Some gloves come with extra padding or reinforcement, especially in the areas most likely to be hit. The non-weapon hand does not require a glove.

Legs

To protect the legs, fencers typically wear long pants made of durable, puncture-resistant material. Fencing knickers, or breeches, are the standard. They are worn with long socks that cover the rest of the leg to below the knee. While the legs are not a common target in sabre fencing, they can still be vulnerable to unintentional hits, so full coverage is important.

Regularly check your gear for any wear and tear and replace items as necessary to ensure they provide maximum protection. It's also important to remember that while safety gear can significantly reduce the risk of injury, it cannot eliminate it entirely. Always spar with control and respect for your partner's safety.

The Position of the Unarmed Hand in Duelling Sabre Fencing

In the intricate dance of sabre fencing, every movement, stance, and position play a pivotal role in determining the outcome of a bout. While much emphasis is placed on the wielding hand and the blade, the position of the unarmed hand, often overlooked, can significantly influence a fencer's strategy, balance, and defence. Delving into the various sabre fencing manuals, we find detailed discussions on the positioning of the unarmed hand, each with its advantages and potential drawbacks.

Punch Touching the Side (Bent Arm Position)

This position encourages the fencer to maintain a straight, vertical stance. By placing the unarmed hand in a punch-like position, either touching the side or slightly behind the body, the fencer is subtly reminded to keep their torso upright. This position emphasizes the movement of the arms and legs, allowing for clear, direct attacks and parries. It can be particularly effective in ensuring that the fencer remains grounded and less prone to leaning or overextending.

Arm bent behind the body (Cantered Arm Position)

With the unarmed hand positioned close to the body's centre of gravity, this stance facilitates rapid torso movements. The fencer can swiftly bend their upper body forward or backward in response to their opponent's actions. This flexibility can be a boon when evading attacks or setting up counterattacks, especially when agility and quick reflexes are paramount.

Natural Position by the Side

This relaxed position allows the unarmed hand to balance the body during rapid movements. However, it does come with a notable vulnerability: the exposure of the unarmed hand to swift weapon swings. While this position offers a natural feel and fluidity in movement, fencers must be wary of their exposed hand, especially against opponents who might exploit this opening.

Interestingly, this position also lends itself to a unique tactic not commonly found in Italian manuals: grabbing the sabre blade with the unarmed hand. While Italian fencing schools don't typically discuss this action, it's a hallmark of other traditions, notably the Polish fencing school. This technique can be a surprising and effective way to control an opponent's blade, though it requires precise timing and execution.

In Conclusion there isn't a "one-size-fits-all" position for the unarmed hand in sabre fencing. The choice largely depends on the fencer's comfort, strategy, and the specific context of the bout. Some fencers might even choose to fluidly transition between these positions within a single assault, adding an element of unpredictability to their strategy. Ultimately, understanding the nuances and potential advantages of each position, as detailed in the fencing manuals, can enrich a fencer's repertoire and adaptability during a duel.

Techniques

Time, Manner, and Measure: The Three Pillars of Fencing and Combat

In every martial art or combat discipline, there are fundamental principles that govern the effectiveness of every technique. In fencing, as in many other martial arts, these principles are embodied by three key concepts: time, manner, and measure. Understanding and mastering these three elements are essential to ensure that every action is executed with precision, effectiveness, and safety.

1. Time

Time, in terms of combat, refers to the right moment to launch an attack or make a defence. It's the ability to perceive and exploit the opponent's openings, acting at the moment when they are most vulnerable and you are least exposed. Fencing literature often emphasizes the importance of time, suggesting that an attack executed at the wrong moment, regardless of its strength or precision, is destined to fail or, worse, expose the fighter to a counterattack.

2. Manner

Manner concerns the correct technique with which an action is executed. Even if you strike at the right time, if the technique is wrong, the attack might not have the desired effect. The correct manner ensures that every movement is efficient, precise, and powerful. Martial literature is rich with examples showing how an imprecise technique can not only fail in its intent but also put the fighter in a disadvantaged position.

3. Measure

Measure refers to the correct distance between you and your opponent. Knowing and controlling this distance is crucial to ensure that every attack reaches its target and that every defence is effective. Too close, and you risk being overwhelmed; too far, and you risk missing the target. Fencing literature often emphasizes the importance of measure, suggesting that the ability to control distance is often what separates an expert fighter from a novice.

The Interconnection of the Three Elements

These three concepts are deeply interconnected. Without the right time, the correct measure might not matter. Without the correct manner, having the right time and measure might not be enough. And without the correct measure, even perfect time and manner might prove ineffective.

In conclusion achieving time, manner, and measure is what makes a technique effective. Missing even just one of these elements can compromise the effectiveness of an attack or defence. As highlighted in martial literature, the ultimate goal of every fighter should be to strike without being struck, and the mastery of time, manner, and measure is essential to achieve this goal.

Salute in duelling Sabre

The salute is an integral part of sabre fencing, signalling respect and readiness between fencers. Whether training or sparring, it's essential to salute as an indication that one is prepared for the bout. A common mistake is to commence the assault when the opponent isn't ready, which can be hazardous. Therefore, it's crucial, especially at the beginning of a bout, to ensure both fencers have exchanged salutes before engaging.

Historically, the salute has deep roots in the traditions of fencing. Beyond its practical purpose, it serves as a gesture of respect, emphasizing the honour and sportsmanship inherent in the duel. It's a silent acknowledgment, saying, "I recognize and respect you as my opponent."

There are various ways to perform the salute, each with its nuances and significance. The author recommends one of the simplest methods described in the Radaelli manual. Starting from the present arm position, raise the armed hand so the blade is vertical on the right side. Then, arc it downward without letting it touch the ground. This broad, non-threatening gesture clearly communicates to the opponent that you're saluting, not initiating an attack. As the hand is raised, the foot on the same side as the armed hand can step forward, adding grace and fluidity to the motion.

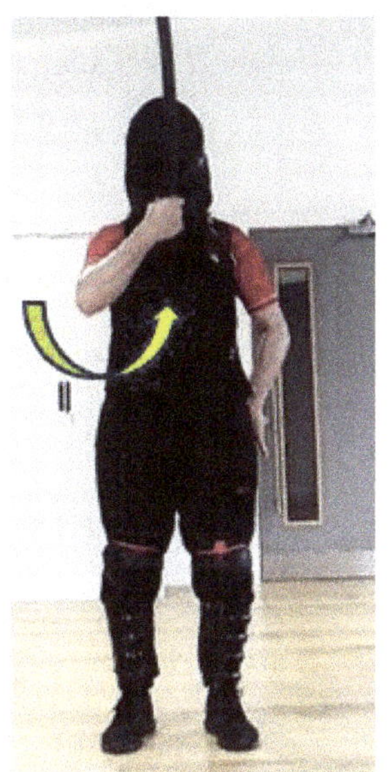

Sabre Grip

The way you grip a sabre is crucial for optimizing its performance in both cuts and thrusts. The back fingers should be positioned close to the bottom of the handle, facilitating the weapon's natural swinging motion. Meanwhile, the thumb should rest on the grip, providing stability and control, especially during thrusting actions.

It's essential that the back of the sabre grip is smooth, as illustrated in the picture below.

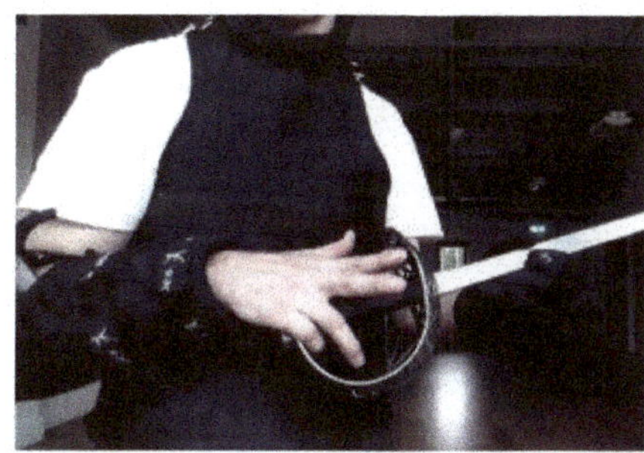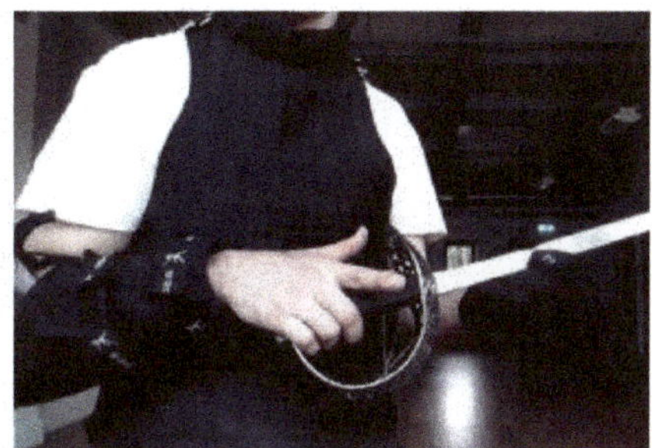

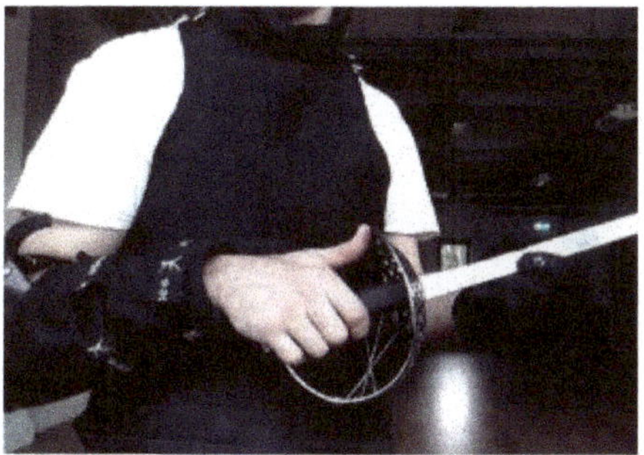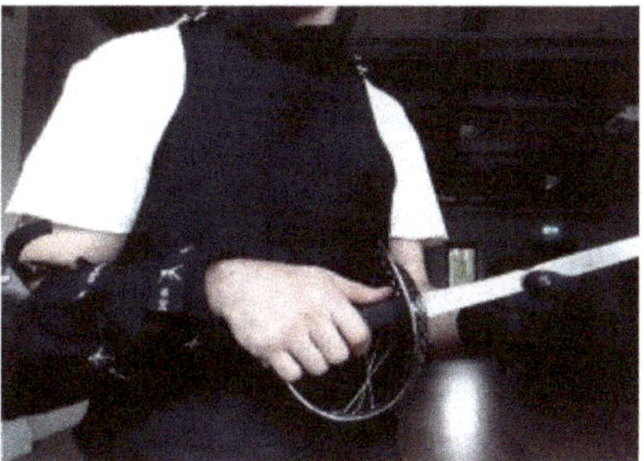

If there's sufficient space, you can adjust your hand closer to the guard. This position offers enhanced control, especially when cutting. When gripped in this manner, the sabre is particularly effective for delivering aggressive cuts. By targeting the opponent's weapon with forceful strikes, you can create openings, capitalizing on the disruptions caused by these powerful blows.

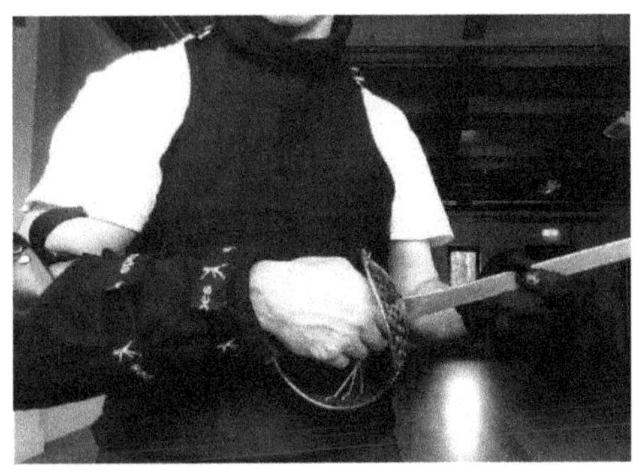

Hand Positions

Understanding hand positions is fundamental to mastering guards and parries in sabre fencing. Think of these positions as rotations of the hand while holding the sabre, akin to the hands of a clock.

There are four primary hand positions, each corresponding to a specific orientation of the blade:

First Position: With the sharp edge of the blade facing upwards, this position aligns with twelve o'clock.

Second Position: Rotate the blade so the sharp edge faces to the right, aligning with three o'clock.

Third Position: The sharp edge now faces downward, corresponding to six o'clock.

Fourth Position: Finally, with the sharp edge facing left, this position aligns with nine o'clock.

For clarity, always ensure the sabre remains parallel to the ground when practicing these positions. The sequence from the first to the fourth position is illustrated in the picture below.

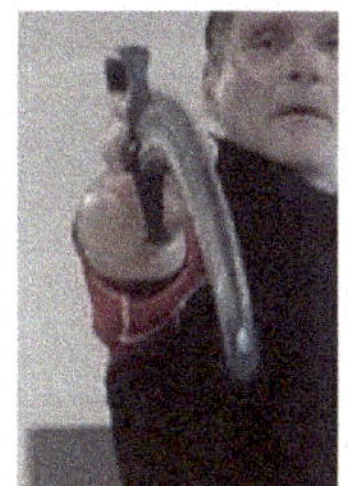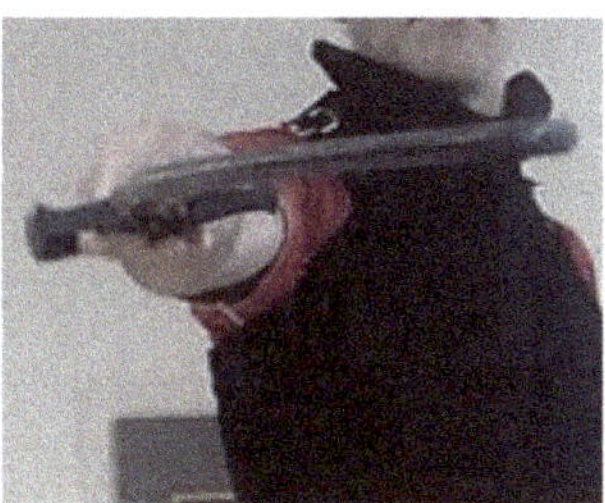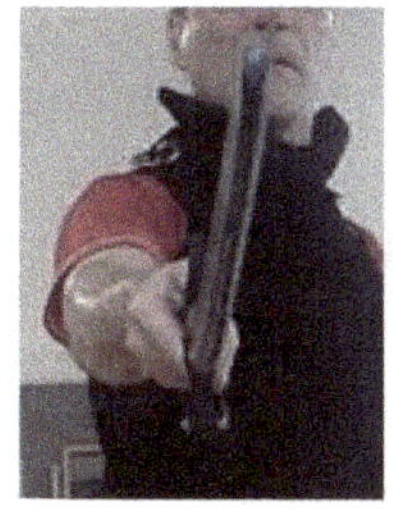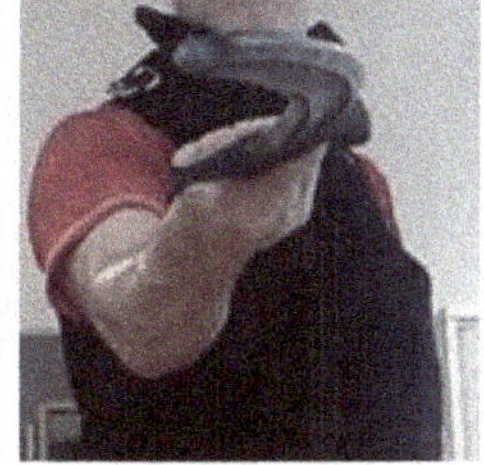

The subsequent image showcases the third position, highlighting the blade's circular motion. When facing this diagram, the fencer shall start from the first position (upside blade) to the fourth clockwise. The mid positions between the 2nd-3rd and 3rd-4th, used for parries, are emphasized in red.

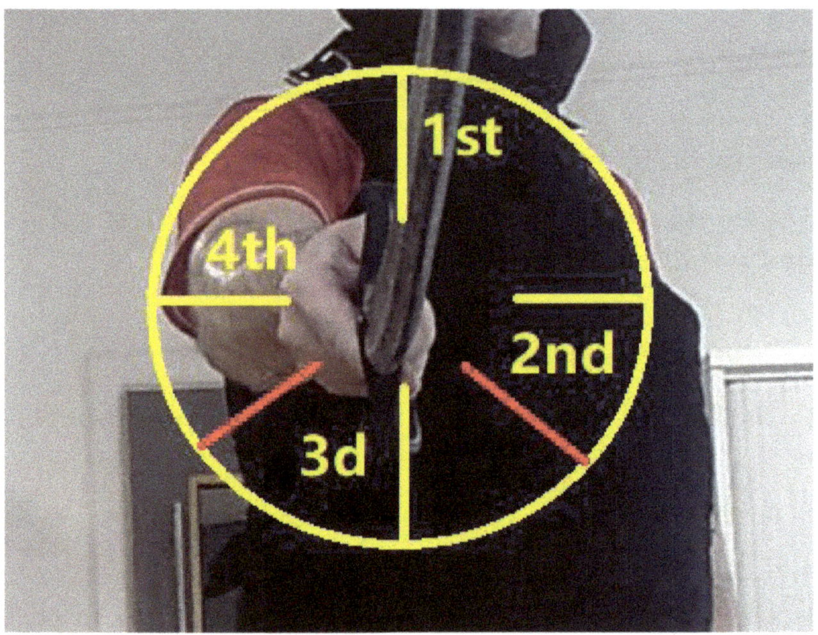

Guards

The guards are the main position from where the fencer can defend and attack, there two only guards, we shall stick with ones mentioned by Parise.

Guard of 1st position

This guard protect the head and shoulders and can be used for cuts to head and thrusts. It can be lowered to protect the lower limbs but in this case the possibility to attack the opponent will reduce.

Guard of 3rd position

This guard protect the body, it's very popular because the arm is quite in rest position and do not make tired the arm as the first guard do. This is less defensive than the first guard but offer better opportunity for offensive actions like thrusts.

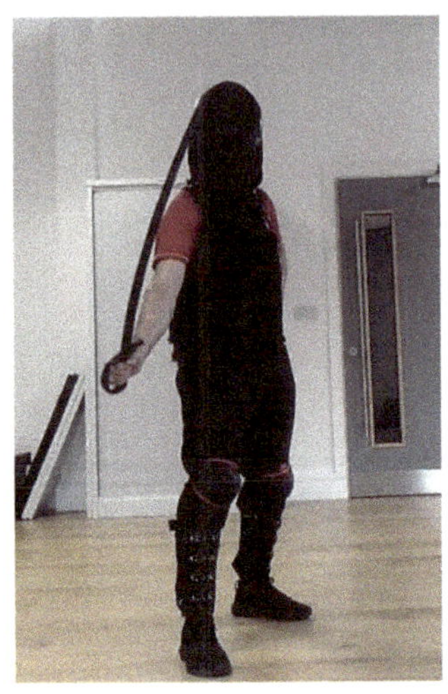

Footwork

Footwork is the foundation of fencing, providing stability, agility, and precision. Here's a breakdown of the essential footwork techniques:

Basic Stance: Your feet should form a 90-degree angle. The front shin must always remain perpendicular to the ground, and the distance between your feet should be approximately half a meter.

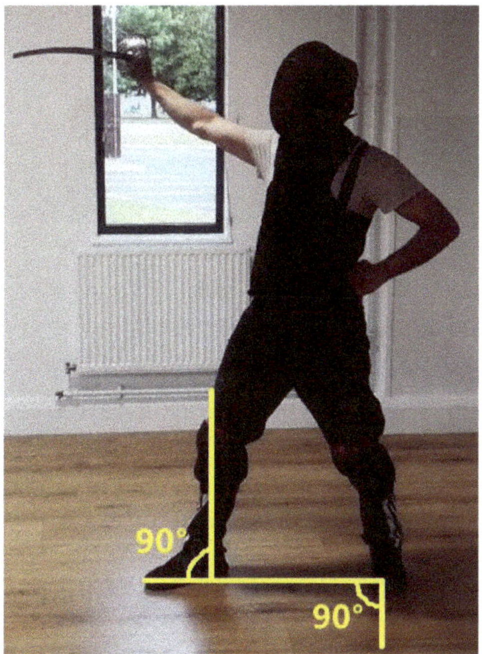

Advancing: When moving forward, lead with the front foot, followed by the back foot. This maintains a consistent distance between your feet, ensuring stability.

Retreating: When moving backward, start with the back foot, then bring the front foot back. This keeps the distance between your feet consistent.

Lateral Movements: Moving to the right, begin with the front foot, followed by the back foot.

Moving to the left, start with the back foot, then follow with the front foot.

The principle here is that the foot closest to the direction of movement initiates the step, ensuring stability.

Jumping Backward: As described in the Radaelli manual, this quick action involves pushing off with the front foot, propelling yourself forward while keeping the sabre stable and pointed at your opponent.

Quick Retreat (Double Step): This is an exception to the standard retreat. The front foot moves behind the back foot, then the back foot follows, re-establishing the half-meter distance. This movement sacrifices some stability for speed and should be used judiciously.

Footwork Exercise: A foundational drill involves taking three steps forward, then three steps backward, followed by three lateral steps to each side. Start slowly, then gradually increase speed. Throughout the exercise, maintain consistent foot spacing and keep the sabre stable, always focusing on the imaginary opponent. As proficiency increases, incorporate the quick retreat into the sequence, alternating it with the standard backward movement.

While these guidelines provide a structured approach to footwork, fencers should adapt and adjust based on their unique strengths, challenges, and fencing style. The goal is to achieve fluidity, responsiveness, and a strong defensive posture, all while keeping the weapon poised for action.

Parries

The sabre, by its very nature, emphasizes dynamic parrying actions as a precursor to launching attacks. Each parrying position not only offers protection against an opponent's strike but also sets the stage for a potential counterattack. While both reference manuals provide insights into parrying, there are subtle differences between them. Here, we'll distil the essence of the seven primary parries, highlighting their correlation with the hand positions previously discussed.

The distinction between a Parry and a Guard position lies in the blade's orientation. In a parry, the blade is extended horizontally, ready to deflect an incoming attack and transition into a countermove.

1 **First Position**: This parry primarily defends against thrusts and cuts aimed at the head. The blade is held horizontally, providing a shield against overhead strikes.

2. **Second Position**: Designed to protect against attacks and thrusts coming from the right side, particularly targeting the body.

3. **Third Position**: With the hand positioned between the 2nd and 3rd stances, this parry's main role is to defend the body from cuts and thrusts originating from the right side.

4. **Fourth Position**: Positioned between the 3rd and 4th stances, this parry primarily defends the fencer's left side from both cuts and thrusts.

5. **Fifth Position**: This parry is essential for guarding against cuts coming from the right side, especially those aimed at the head.

6. **Sixth Position**: A mirror to the fifth, this parry is designed to protect the head from cuts coming from the left side.

7. **Seventh Position**: Resembling the sixth but with a vertically oriented blade, this parry's main function is to shield the right side of the body from cuts.

Attack

In sabre fencing, the manner in which you approach and attack your opponent can vary widely. Below are foundational techniques that fencers can use as a basis to develop more advanced and nuanced attacks:

1. **Direct Hit**: This involves a straightforward attack on an exposed target, be it the head, body, or limbs. The most frequent targets are cuts to the opponent's armed arm, as it's often the most forward and accessible. A cut from the 3rd stance can transition to the 4th, targeting the inner side of the arm. If the outer side of the arm is exposed, a cut from the 3rd position can shift to the 2nd. The head or torso can be targeted from the 1st position, transitioning either to the 2nd or 4th. A direct vertical cut to the head can be executed from the 3rd position. Leg cuts are effective from the 1st or 3rd position, transitioning to the 2nd to target the opponent's back leg or to the 4th for the front leg. The lunge, a foundational move, involves extending the legs, pushing off with the back foot, ensuring the front leg remains perpendicular to the ground, and fully extending the armed arm to maximize reach. The lunge thrust is typically executed with the hand in the 2nd position. Notably, rising cuts, executed with an upward blade rotation or "Moulinet," can effectively target an opponent's limbs.

Direct vertical cut to head

Direct horizontal cut to head

 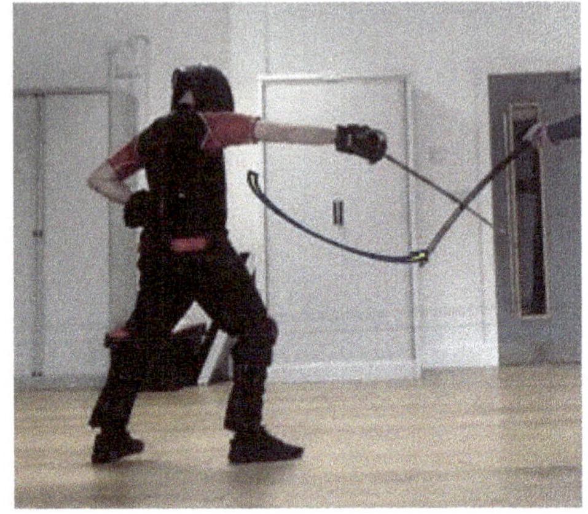

Lunge

2. **Feint and Strike**: A classic deceptive move, the fencer initiates a horizontal cut (from the 3rd or 4th position) towards the head or body, but swiftly alters it to a vertical cut in the 3rd position. This feint can also transition into a thrust in the 2nd position.

3. **Weapon Engagement**: A strategic move in sabre fencing involves forcefully striking the opponent's blade. A common tactic is to engage the opponent's weapon with a robust cut in the 3rd position, followed by a forward step and a subsequent cut in the 4th position.

4. **The Parry Yield**: This advanced technique is often employed by seasoned fencers. It involves actively parrying an attack and intentionally bending the armed arm to create an opening for a counterattack. For instance, when an opponent delivers a strong overhead cut from the left, the fencer can parry in the 5th position and then subtly bend the arm to lower the opponent's weapon. This creates an opening for a leftward Moulinet targeting the opponent's head. A similar strategy can be employed when parrying in the 7th position against an attack to the right side of the head or arm. A slight arm drop can set up a rightward Moulinet to the opponent's head.

Yield from the 6th position

These foundational techniques provide a roadmap for fencers to develop their unique style and strategies. Mastery of these basics can lead to more advanced and effective combat manoeuvres in sabre fencing.

Moulinets

Moulinets, characterized by their sweeping, circular motions, are foundational to sabre fencing. These techniques are designed to deliver powerful cuts to an opponent's head, body, or limbs. Additionally, moulinets can be employed to strike an opponent's weapon, either to disarm or to create an opening for a direct hit. Initially, fencers learn moulinets in three distinct stages. However, with practice, these stages merge into a singular, fluid motion that's both swift and precise.

There are three primary categories of moulinet cuts: those targeting the head, the body, and the uppercut variations. Detailed illustrations of these movements, both from frontal and lateral perspectives, can be found in subsequent chapters.

1. **Left to Head**: This moulinet aims to strike the left side of an opponent's head. The sabre's point initially dips downward, tracing a semi-circle, before rising sharply to complete the cut.

Left to Head, Lateral view

2. **Right to Head**: Mirroring the Left to Head moulinet, this movement follows the same trajectory but targets the right side of the opponent's head.

3. **Left to Body**: Targeting the left side of an opponent's torso, this moulinet begins with the sabre's point elevated. The blade then descends in a circular motion, culminating in a cut to the body.

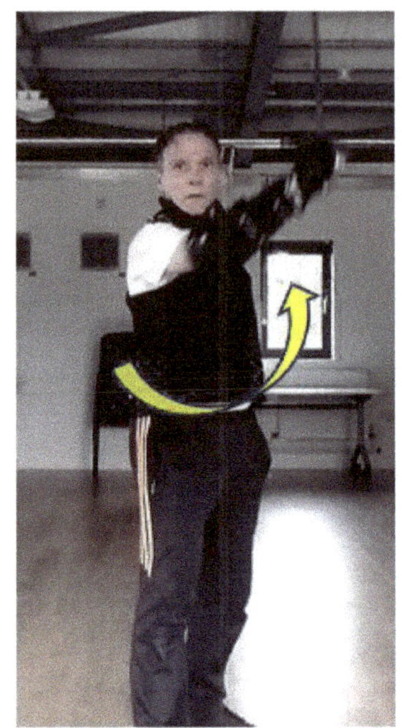

4. **Right to Body**: A counterpart to the Left to Body moulinet, this technique targets the right side of the opponent's torso.

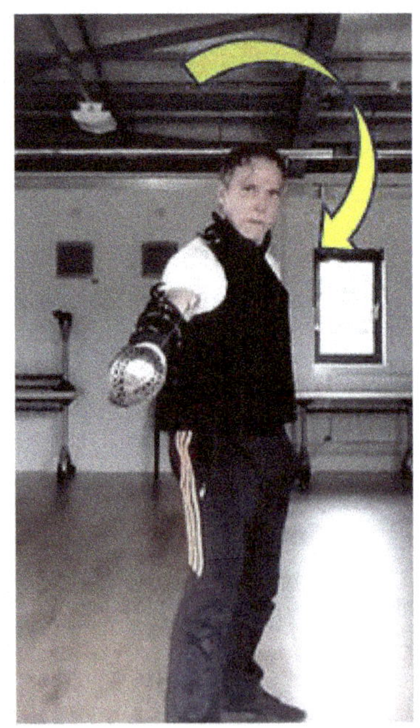

5. **Left Uppercut**: This variant begins with the sabre's point lowered towards the ground. The blade then arcs upwards in a swift, uppercut motion, aiming for the right side of the opponent's body.

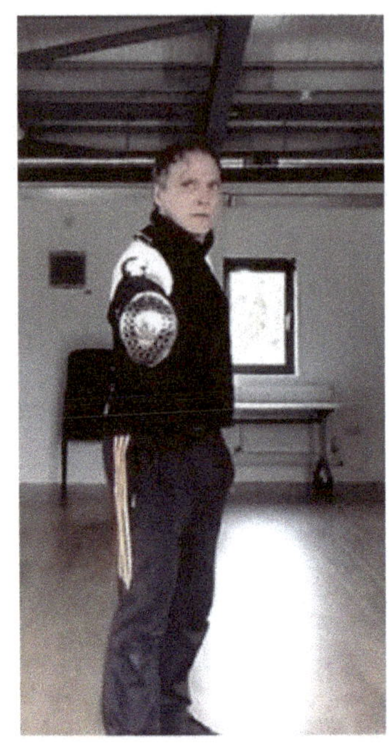
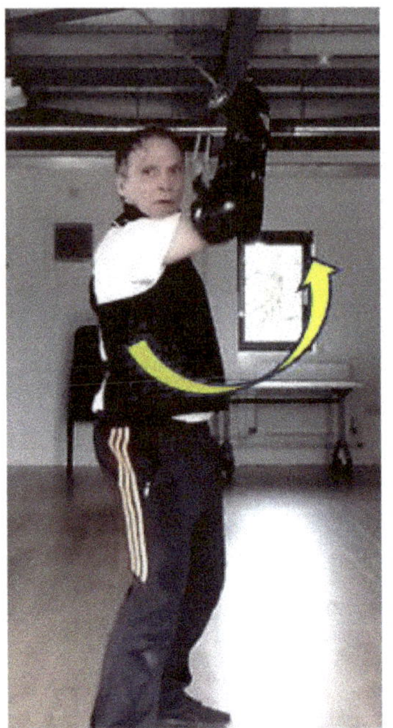

6. **Right Uppercut**: A mirror to the Left Uppercut, this moulinet targets the left side of the opponent's body.

Understanding Timing in Attacks

1. **Attacking in Time**: This strategy revolves around seizing the opportune moment to strike your opponent when they least expect it. It involves launching a direct attack when the opponent is unprepared, either because they're momentarily distracted or transitioning into a guard position. Recognizing these vulnerable moments requires keen observation and quick reflexes. For instance, if an opponent is shifting their stance or taking a lateral step, it might be the perfect time to strike.

2. **Counter-Timing Attack**: This is a reactive strategy. As your opponent initiates an assault, you take a step back to create distance and then immediately launch a counterattack. This exploits the brief window when the opponent is overextended or off-balance from their initial attack, making it harder for them to defend against your counter.

3. **Simultaneous Attack**: This tactic involves countering your opponent's move with an immediate assault of your own. As they begin their attack, you simultaneously launch your strike. The goal is to catch them off-guard, as they're committed to their offensive move and might not be prepared to defend against your simultaneous attack.

Understanding Lethal and Significant Wounds

This paragraph will discuss the importance of lethal and significant wounds in duelling sabre fencing, detailing how to recognize and deliver these strikes while adhering to safety guidelines.

Lethal Wounds: Definition and Techniques

In the context of duelling sabre fencing, lethal wounds are injuries that would result in the immediate end of a fight, typically targeting vital organs such as the lungs, heart, neck, and head. The primary goal of fencers in this martial art is to survive, so landing a lethal wound is of utmost importance.

When practicing, a lethal strike should cause the blade to bend completely, simulating a realistic hit. A mere touch is not enough; the weapon must hit fully to be considered a valid hit. However, it is important to remember that after receiving a lethal wound, the opponent is still considered to be fighting for a couple of seconds, representing the time it would take for the wound to incapacitate them in a real-life scenario.

Thrusts are the preferred technique for targeting the body, as cuts are generally not lethal in most cases. For cuts to be effective, they must be delivered to the neck or head with a clear-cutting movement. Both thrusts and cuts can be valid techniques for targeting the head, but only if the weapon hit significantly the opponent, indicating a realistic hit.

Significant Wounds: Definition and Techniques

In addition to lethal wounds, duelling sabre fencing also recognizes significant wounds. These are injuries that may not be fatal but can severely impair the opponent's ability to fight effectively. One such significant wound is a strike to the armed hand, which can force the opponent to switch the weapon to their other hand.

A valid significant wound in this context would be a cut to the inside of the wrist, where the tendons controlling hand movement are located. A severed tendon would render the hand incapable of holding a weapon.

Visualizing Lethal and Significant Wounds

To better understand the locations of lethal and significant wounds on the human body, refer to the accompanying picture, where the target areas are marked in red. This visualization will help fencers develop a mental map of critical points to target during practice and competition.

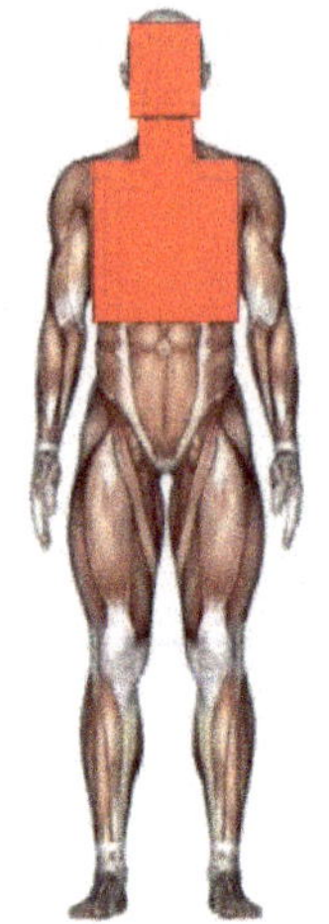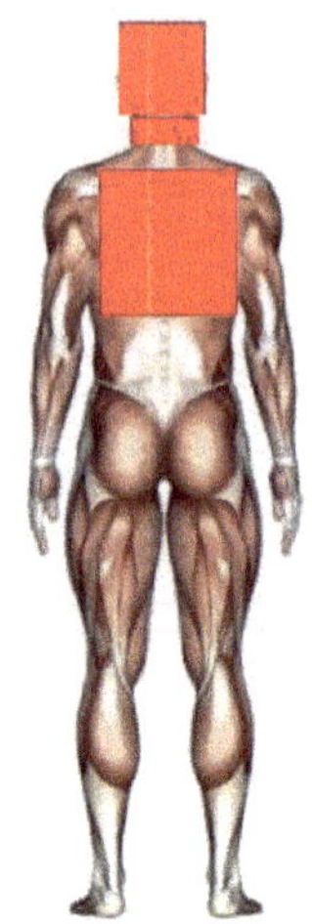

Here below typical hits (crosses) and cuts (line) of Sabre fencing.

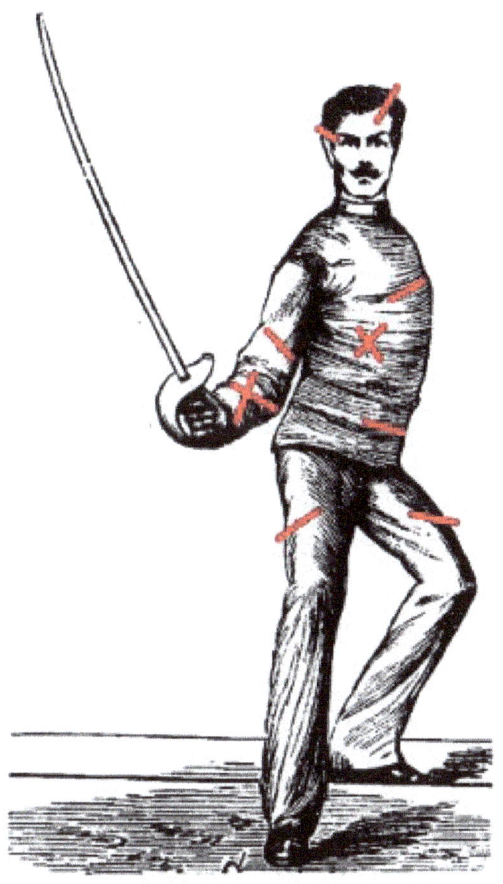

Types of Fighters in Duelling Sabre Fencing: Aggressive and Defensive

Introduction

Understanding an opponent's fighting style is essential for success in duelling sabre fencing. Recognizing and adapting to different types of fighters can provide a significant advantage in a match. In this chapter, we will discuss the two main types of fighters – aggressive and defensive – and how to effectively engage with each type during a duel. We will also explore the importance of adapting one's own tactics and techniques to counter various opponents and strategies.

Aggressive Fighters

Aggressive fighters in sabre fencing tend to rely on powerful attacks, seeking to overwhelm their opponents with their strength and assertiveness. They generally prefer close-distance combat and will attempt to engage in rapid exchanges with their adversaries. At the beginning of a duel, aggressive fighters can be difficult to control, as their unpredictable and forceful movements can catch an opponent off-guard.

To counter aggressive fighters, it is essential to maintain a safe distance and anticipate, in time, their attacks. By staying out of their preferred range, you can force them to take risks and make mistakes. Surviving the first few assaults is critical, as aggressive fighters often reveal their techniques and tendencies early in the duel. Once you have a clear understanding of their approach, it becomes easier to exploit their weaknesses and land effective hits.

Defensive Fighters

Defensive fighters, on the other hand, tend to be more cautious and deliberate in their movements. They often keep their distance from opponents, waiting for the right moment to strike. Their strategy typically involves using a variety of techniques to confuse and outmanoeuvre their adversaries, making them more challenging to face as the duel progresses.

To combat defensive fighters, it is crucial to remain close to them and adopt a defensive stance. Staying within their comfort zone can disrupt their strategy and force them to adapt. By focusing on defence rather than aggression, you can confuse them and create opportunities for counterattacks.

Adapting Tactics and Techniques

While recognizing and responding to an opponent's fighting style is important, the most successful sabre fencers are those who can adapt their tactics and techniques according to the situation. Being able to switch between aggressive and defensive modes, as well as employing a variety of strategies, can keep an opponent guessing and make it difficult for them to predict your actions.

Incorporating advanced tactical techniques, as discussed in the dedicated chapter, can provide an even greater advantage in sabre fencing. By mastering a range of skills and approaches, a fencer can effectively counter various types of fighters and increase their chances of success in a duel.

The Sabre's Universal Techniques: A Foundation for Multiple Weapons Training

The art of fencing, while often categorized by the specific weapon in use, is underpinned by a set of universal principles and techniques that transcend individual disciplines. The sabre, with its unique blend of agility, power, and precision, embodies many of these foundational concepts, making its study beneficial for practitioners of various weapons.

Shared Techniques Across Weapons

At its core, the sabre emphasizes the importance of fluidity in movement, continuous slashing actions, and the ability to keep an opponent engaged defensively. These principles are not exclusive to the sabre but are echoed in the techniques of other weapons:

Swords: Traditional straight swords, while often associated with thrusting, also employ slashing techniques. The footwork, distance management, and timing learned from sabre training can significantly enhance a swordsman's repertoire.

Sticks Stick combat, or stick fighting, shares the sabre's emphasis on continuous movement and engagement. The slashing motions of the sabre are mirrored in the swinging strikes of a stick, and the defensive parries and evasions are conceptually similar.

Knives and Daggers: Knife fighting, given the weapon's shorter length, demands close attention to distance and timing, much like sabre fencing. The wrist's flexibility and the ability to deliver rapid slashes are techniques that both knife fighters and sabrists must master.

The Sabre's Unique Contributions

The sabre's emphasis on continuous slashing actions is a defining feature. By keeping the weapon in constant motion, a sabrist can maintain offensive pressure, forcing their opponent to remain defensive and react to a barrage of attacks. This concept of sustained aggression can be beneficially applied to other weapons, teaching practitioners the value of seizing the initiative and controlling the tempo of an engagement.

Furthermore, the sabre places a premium on wrist flexibility and precision. The weapon's curve and design necessitate a range of intricate wrist movements for both offense and defence. This focus on the wrist's mobility and strength is invaluable, especially for weapons that require finesse and rapid directional changes, such as knives or short swords.

Cross-Training Benefits

Training with the sabre offers a holistic approach to fencing that can be applied across various disciplines. For instance:

Polearms: Weapons like the spear or halberd, while longer, benefit from the sabre's teachings on distance management and timing.

Rapiers: While rapiers emphasize thrusting, the footwork and distance management techniques from sabre training can enhance a rapier fencer's agility and positioning.

In conclusion the sabre, while a distinct and storied weapon in its own right, serves as a foundational tool for understanding the broader principles of fencing and combat. Its techniques, emphasizing fluidity, continuous engagement, and wrist precision, offer invaluable lessons for practitioners of various weapons. By mastering the sabre, one not only becomes proficient with this particular weapon but also gains insights and skills that enhance proficiency across a spectrum of martial disciplines.

Five Italian Sabre Duels

Sure, here are five accounts of duels involving the Italian duelling sabre during the second half of the 19th century:

1. **The Duel of Honour**: In the bustling city of Milan, two well-known fencing masters, Signor Luigi and Signor Roberto, found themselves in a disagreement over a point of technique. Both masters were so convinced of their correctness that they agreed to settle the matter through a duel. They met at dawn in a secluded park, each armed with an Italian duelling sabre. The duel was tense and prolonged, as each master showed great skill and respect for the other. Eventually, Signor Luigi managed to land a hit on Signor Roberto's arm, proving his point. The duel ended with a handshake and newfound respect for each other's abilities.

2. **The Artist's Challenge**: In the scenic town of Florence, a young artist named Antonio found himself challenged to a duel by a jealous rival, Pietro, who accused Antonio of stealing his artistic ideas. Despite having no formal training, Antonio had always been fascinated by fencing and practiced with his friends using wooden sticks. The duel took place at sunset near the Arno River. Against all odds, Antonio's natural talent and quick reflexes allowed him to disarm Pietro and win the duel. The experience inspired Antonio to study fencing formally, adding a new layer to his art.

3. **The Duel for Love**: In the romantic city of Venice, two suitors, Count Marco and Duke Lorenzo, found themselves in love with the same woman, the beautiful and elusive Contessa Bianca. To settle the matter, they decided to duel for her hand. They met on a secluded island in the Venetian lagoon,

under the watchful eyes of their seconds. After an intense exchange, Count Marco landed a superficial cut on Duke Lorenzo's shoulder, winning the duel. Contessa Bianca, moved by Marco's courage, accepted his hand in marriage.

4. **The Soldier's Victory**: In the military city of Turin, Captain Giovanni, a decorated soldier, was challenged to a duel by a fellow officer, Lieutenant Franco, over a perceived slight. Despite Franco's fiery temper and aggressive style, Giovanni's cool-headedness and precision with the Italian duelling sabre allowed him to parry Franco's wild attacks and deliver a decisive touch to Franco's chest. The duel served as a lesson in humility for Franco and reaffirmed Giovanni's reputation as a formidable fencer.

5. **The Merchant's Triumph**: In the bustling port of Genoa, a wealthy merchant named Enrico was insulted by a nobleman, Signor Alfredo, who looked down on those who earned their wealth through trade. Enraged by the insult, Enrico challenged Alfredo to a duel. Despite Alfredo's formal fencing training, Enrico's determination and cunning strategy allowed him to land a touch on Alfredo's leg, winning the duel and earning him the grudging respect of the nobility.

Bibliography

Parise, M. (1884). *Trattato Tecnico Pratico Della Scherma di Spada e Sciabola.* Roma: Tipografia Nazionale.

Radaelli, G. (1885). *Istruzione per la Scherma di Sciabola e Spada.* Milano: Fratelli DUMOLARD Editori.

Appendix

Giovanni's Martial Arts background

Giovanni is an instructor at the Culham Historical Fencing and Mixed Martial Arts Club (CSSA) in the UK, with a diverse martial arts background. His martial arts journey started in 1991 with Japanese Karate (kumite). He then moved on to Kickboxing for six years and later Muay Thai for four years, actively participating in amateur competitions.

His training took a historical turn in 1999 when he was introduced to Medieval and Renaissance fencing by his master of Italian historical fencing. He started training in the manual of Fiore de Liberi and Marozzo. His interest in historical martial arts led him to join a group that trained in ancient Olympic boxing (Pygmachia), wrestling (Pale), the ancient mixed martial art of Pankration, and gladiatura in an experimental archaeology style (Arsdimicandi).

In 2000, Giovanni earned his first qualification as an Instructor of Medieval Fencing, which was soon followed by a second one in Renaissance Fencing (IRSAST). Even before receiving these qualifications, he had begun teaching his first class in southern Italy. His mastery of different disciplines led him to earn another qualification as an instructor of modern Pankration (Athlima), after which he taught his first class of bare hand fighting in northern Italy, specifically in Venice. Alongside his students in northern and southern Italy, Giovanni participated in historical tournaments and battles. He later moved to South Milan, where he established two classes focusing on bare-hand fighting and fencing.

In 2013, Giovanni expanded his martial arts repertoire by gaining a qualification as a mixed martial arts instructor (FIGMMA). To further broaden his skill set, he joined a local club focused on defensive and dynamic shooting with firearms, actively participating in competitions.

In 2018, his career took him to China, but he continued to instruct students in all of his disciplines, including boxing. After relocating to England, he joined a local historical fencing school in Wiltshire, followed by the Hema Fencing school in Oxford (OSS), and a Brazilian Ju Jitsu school to improve his wrestling skills.

Giovanni's martial arts qualifications were validated by the British Martial Arts and Boxing Association (BMABA) in 2022.

In 2023, Giovanni further honed his martial arts expertise. That same year, he earned his first prized stripe in the German longsword style and imparted his knowledge of Italian martial arts by conducting an intensive course on Traditional Italian Knife techniques in Oxford. He has authored two martial arts books: "European Martial Arts," which provides an overview of various fighting techniques ranging from hand-to-hand combat to fencing and firearms, and "Italian Knife Fencing," which delves into the traditional knife fencing techniques prevalent in Italy during the early 20th century.

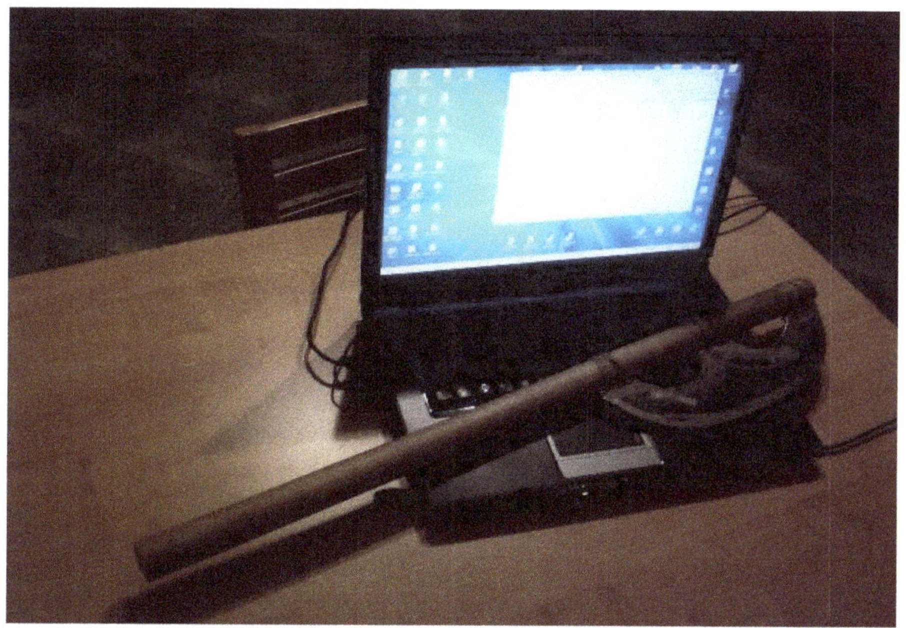

Giovanni's Expertise and Offerings

Giovanni is a seasoned instructor with a diverse skill set in various martial arts and weapons training. Based in England, he specializes in offering tailored sessions to meet the unique needs and interests of his students.

Whether you're a beginner looking to delve into the world of martial arts or an advanced practitioner seeking to refine your skills, Giovanni's expertise covers a broad spectrum. His lessons encompass traditional Italian weapons like the Longsword, Polearm, and Duelling Sabre, as well as the art of Traditional Italian Knife Fencing. For those interested in bare hands martial arts, Giovanni also provides training in Pankration, Mixed Martial Arts and Muay Thai.

To schedule a personalized lesson, class, or workshop with Giovanni, you can reach out to him directly via email at john154326@gmail.com. Whatever your martial arts aspirations, Giovanni is equipped to guide you on your journey.